# KIRKHAM

## NORTH Y...

❖

### Stuart Harrison

Dormitory

Latrine

Chapel

Chapter house

South transept

Guest house

Kitchen

Refectory

*The striking ruins of Kirkham Priory in North Yorkshire have a fascinating history. This community of Augustinian priors survived an early attempt to transfer them to the more widespread Cistercian order. The size and wealth of the Priory rivalled some of the more famous nearby Cistercian houses such as Rievaulx Abbey.*

*During the thirteenth century, the priory prospered under the patronage of the de Roos lords of Helmsley, whose heraldry can be seen elaborately carved into the facade of the gatehouse, and there were several phases of building that can still be traced in the detail of the extensive ruins.*

*This guidebook offers a richly-illustrated guided tour, explaining the main features of the remains of the priory buildings, as well as a lively anecdotal history.*

# ❖ CONTENTS ❖

*Published by English Heritage , 23 Savile Row, London W1X 1AB*
*© English Heritage 2000   First published by English Heritage 2000*
*Photographs by English Heritage Photographic Unit and copyright*
*of English Heritage, unless otherwise stated.*

*Edited by Louise Wilson*
*Designed by Pauline Hull. Plans by Hardlines*
*Printed by Snoeck-Ducaju & Zoon, Belgium*
*C60  3/00  FA4754  ISBN 1 85074 728 8*

# TOUR OF THE PRIORY

Kirkham Priory is picturesquely sited on a slope of the east bank of the River Derwent. This situation restricted the development of the buildings, some of which had to be terraced into the hillside. The site is entered through a splendid gatehouse of late thirteenth- or early fourteenth-century date. It is flanked by a porter's lodge and other chambers which may have served as guest-houses or the site of the priory courthouse. Between the gatehouse and the church there is a large open area of grass which was formerly the outer court. Though there is now no trace of any buildings, aerial photographs quite clearly show the outline of a large hall complex to the north of the church. Presumably this formed extensive guest accommodation and may have been provided for the use of important patrons.

*Aerial photograph of Kirkham Priory looking north*

*Start your tour at the church, by walking north-eastwards across the grass towards ruined walls with the remaining tall fragments of the east wall at the far end.*

ENGLISH HERITAGE/SKYSCAN BALLOON PHOTOGRAPHY

*The remains of a tall window at the east end of the church*

*Details of the western doorway leading from the nave to the cloister*

*The west end of the church and the vaulted outer parlour*

## CHURCH

The church is much ruined and, apart from sections at the east and west ends, is reduced to low walls. However, enough survives to establish the main building sequences and what the building must have looked like.

Initially, the canons built a modest church without an aisle. Adjoining it on the south side was a square cloister court, around which were the main domestic buildings of the priory. In about 1170, the church was extensively rebuilt, though some parts of the original building were retained, so that the cloister was not disturbed. These walls were thickened and heightened, and, because they are now ruined, show both periods of building quite clearly, and the vertical joint between the two. The rebuilt church had new, enlarged piers at the crossing, and probably a central tower above. Like the contemporary church at Gisborough Priory, it also had the unusual feature of a second tower at the west end.

From the fragmentary remains, the western tower appears to have had a large recess on its west side, with the superstructure carried on a

large arch above. The tower was open towards the nave, with a large arch and, unlike most other churches, there was no main west doorway. The main entrance seems to have been in the north wall of the nave, where the very lowest part of it still survives. Opposite this entrance doorway, in the south wall of the nave, was another splendid doorway which formed an entrance to the cloister. This would normally have been kept locked, but would have been used by the canons to enter the nave for the weekly Sunday processions. Unfortunately it is also badly ruined, but retains more of its surround intact.

Until the construction of a separate chapel for the parishioners, the nave was used as the parish church. The worshipping parishioners were separated from the choir by a rood screen, below which were two doors which the canons could lock. Fifteenth-century documents mention a font and a bell tower and say that the parishioners were responsible for the upkeep of the bells and bell-ropes. Parishioners were also encouraged to use a chapel located outside the abbey gates, which was served by a secular chaplain. Several reasons for this were given: that the canons should not be disturbed during their services; that in a time of plague, infection should not be brought into the monastery, and that it was more convenient for the parishioners.

At the east end of the nave are the remains of the stone base of the screen which divided the parochial nave (where the local people worshipped) from the canons' part of the church.

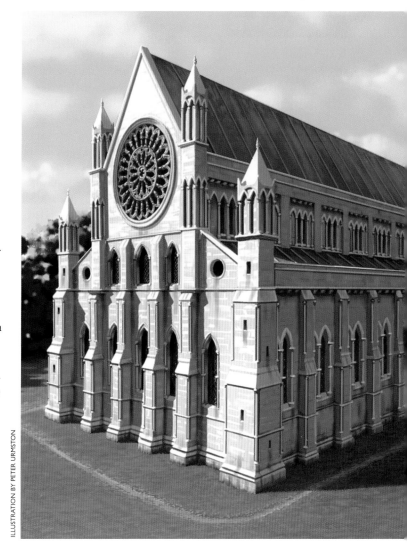

*Reconstruction drawing of the impressive east end of the Priory church as it would have looked in the thirteenth century.*

ILLUSTRATION BY PETER URMSTON

*Lead ventilator grill used within a stained glass window in the church*

*Detail of the elaborate stone carving around the window arch at the far end of the presbytery*

Beyond the screen is a second doorway which survived unaltered from the first church, as the primitive details of its surround quite clearly show.

*Walk up the length of the nave to the crossing (the point at which it meets the two side-arms).*

In the crossing, under the central tower, there were once timber choir-stalls in which the canons sat during the main services. On either side of the tower, the transepts or side-arms of the cross shape had chapels on the east side, where the bases of the piers which supported their arched entrances can still be seen. The original choir did not have an aisle, and was extended eastwards in the first rebuilding.

*Continue from the crossing towards the east end.*

## Presbytery

In the thirteenth century, the canons embarked on another scheme to re-build the whole church, but only completed a vast new presbytery (the eastern part containing the altar) before the money ran out. The new building was constructed of high-quality ashlar (stone blocks), in contrast to the earlier buildings, which were of coursed rubblestone with ashlar dressings. However, the earlier buildings were plastered. Old and new would have been painted externally and internally with white limewash, so that the difference between them would not have been as obvious as it is now.

*Viscera box excavated at Kirkham, probably used to bury the internal organs of the deceased de Roos lords of Helmsley*

*Two axe heads found during excavation at Kirkham*

What remains of the splendid new thirteenth-century building are low walls and parts of its eastern windows. The surviving details show that it had arcades of eight bays and was richly decorated with carved capitals and pointed lancet windows. Eighteenth-century drawings of the east wall, when it was more complete, show that it had two tiers of such windows with a huge circular window above them, similar to that in the south transept of York Minster (see page 5). In size and style it would have looked very similar to the contemporary presbytery at Rievaulx but with more lavish decoration. It must have been one of the most architecturally impressive buildings in the north of England.

Along the east wall was a series of chapels, and the high altar was set back two bays to the west of these. Around it, and beneath the arches of the main arcades, were buried the patrons of the Priory, the de Roos lords of Helmsley. Amongst the finds recovered when the site was excavated, was a small stone box complete with its lid, which probably served as the depository for the preserved viscera or internal organs of one of the burials. There was also part of a splendid late thirteenth-century shrine or screen with miniature geometric tracery and gilded pinnacles.

During the excavation of the site, the foundations of the east walls of the earlier presbytery were also discovered about halfway down the later presbytery. Two rows of stone markers in the grass show their positions. Though the great thirteenth-century scheme to rebuild the whole church was abandoned, some additional construction was carried out. In the fourteenth century, a chapel was added to the south aisle, and a stone tomb slab can still be seen set against its south wall, and an altar base against the east. Similar small-scale additions were also made on each side of the north transept. Structures on the west and north sides were probably vestries for storing the books, plate and vestments used in the services. On its east side an enlarged chapel was also built out against the north aisle of the presbytery. Both the added chapels may have been provided as private chantries, and burial spaces for the saying of mass in memory of particular patrons.

*Return to the crossing and enter the cloister to the left of the nave.*

ENGLISH HERITAGE/SKYSCAN BALLOON PHOTOGRAPHY

*Aerial view showing the square cloister court with the cherry tree in blossom*

*Mirror case found at Kirkham, probably dropped by a visitor*

## CLOISTER

The cloister is a rectangular court which formerly had a covered alley on each side, though all trace of these has now vanished. The alley roofs would probably have been supported on open arches, and may have been embellished with animal and figure sculptures as they were in other Augustinian priories. The central court or garth might have been laid out as a formal garden which sometimes, like the priories at Norton and Haverfordwest, had water running through open drain channels around the sides. When not attending services in the church, the canons spent most of their day in this court. In the north alley (backing onto the nave) they would have been provided with a series of carrels or desks at which they might study or write. On the east side of the cloister (to your left as you enter) there is a slype or passage adjoining the church, and a small narrow room with a stone bench which may have served as the parlour. This was the only place that the canons could hold conversation - there was a rule of silence in the rest of the cloister court. The range of buildings on the east side of the court included the chapter house and dormitory, while the south range included the refectory.

*Turning left, move southwards down the east range of cloister buildings. Look into the narrow parlour (the first room on your left) and then turn left up the steps into the larger room next to it.*

## CHAPTER HOUSE

This is the chapter house. It was here that the canons met daily to discuss business, confess faults and receive discipline for any errors they had committed. As the floor level of the chapter house was above the cloister, there was a short flight of steps up into the room. It was entered from the cloister through a central doorway, which was sub-divided into two by a slender pier, traces of which remain. Though the building is much ruined, the remains show that it was a very large room of thirteenth-century date, with carved arches, and benches all round the side walls, of which only the bases now remain. It was probably covered in a single span with stone ribbed vaulting. Eventually the weight of the vault seems to have spread the south wall which was reinforced by strengthening the buttresses and remarkably, though the original buttress has disappeared, a large section of this added masonry still survives. When the chapter house was rebuilt, it was set further east than its predecessor, indicating that there was an intention to rebuild the whole of the east side of the cloister to a new plan.

*Move to the canons' dormitory which extends south from the chapter house.*

## Dormitory

Normally the canons' dormitory would have been at first-floor level, with a staircase in the south transept for access to the church for night services, but at Kirkham, it was set at the level of the cloister, because of the fall of the ground to the south. The southern half was supported on a vaulted undercroft of five double bays with a central row of piers. At its south end can be seen the high wall of the latrine or reredorter which still stands almost to eaves level. The holes that can be clearly seen are the doorways from the dormitory, with a lamp niche set between them, though one doorway has since been blocked to accommodate a chimney flue. These show that originally there was a one-way system of entrance and exit to the reredorter.

*The steps leading up from the cloister to the chapter house*

*View of the upper part of the dormitory wall showing doorway and lamp niches*

*The decorated doorway leading from the cloister to the refectory*

*Right: Detail of tap with bird on handle found at Kirkham*

*The tracery panelling of the late 13th-century arched laver*

*Return to the cloister and turn right down its south side.*

At the far (west) end of the south alley there is a fine, late twelfth-century doorway which formed the entrance to the refectory. It is highly decorated with various forms of chevron or zigzag ornament. In the south-west corner the remains of a spiral staircase can be seen, which once gave access to the undercroft below the refectory.

*Turn right again into the west alley.*

## Laver

Adjoining the spiral staircase, as you turn into the west cloister, are two large arched recesses, of late thirteenth-century date, with splendid geometric tracery panelling on the rear wall. These arches formed the laver, where the canons washed their hands before entering the refectory. It

was also used weekly and on Maundy Thursday, when the prior washed the feet of the canons in emulation of Christ washing the feet of the disciples before the Last Supper. There was a piped water supply with taps, sited over a trough, and chases for the pipes can be seen on the other (south) side.

*Move on up the west side of the cloister.*

## THE WEST BUILDING RANGE

Just beyond the laver is a doorway which gave access to the western range of domestic buildings. This may also have been the doorway to the warming house – a communal room with a warm fire in winter – where those canons studying in the unheated cloister might go to warm themselves.

In this west wall a series of small square holes, known as putlogs, can also be seen. These were provided for the scaffold poles used during construction.

In the far north-west corner is the outer parlour which formed the main entrance to the cloister complex. It was vaulted in two bays and retains some of its unusual six-part stone

*The outline of vaulting on the rear of the west cloister wall*

vaulting of Early Gothic date, supported by shafts with waterleaf capitals. Above the vault there may have been a first-floor chapel, and there are traces of shafts with corbels (little supports) on the south wall which would have held the floor.

*Pass through the parlour and turn left.*

As you walk southwards from the parlour, it is possible to appreciate how these buildings on the west side of the cloister were heavily terraced and supported on stone vaults which remain outlined against the surviving walls.

*At the end of the west range turn left to view the refectory.*

*Detail of the vaulted entrance to the cloister, showing the doorway column with its waterleaf capital*

*The vaulted entrance to the cloister with the remains of a chapel above*

*View of the refectory from the south-east*

*A 16th-century spoon found at Kirkham*

*View of the kitchen from the north-east*

## Refectory

The refectory also stood on a vaulted undercroft, supported on a central row of piers, traces of which can still be seen. This side of the refectory doorway dates from the thirteenth century, and is flanked by the remains of a cupboard for storing the cutlery and plates. Along the north wall are a series of vertical slots for a wall arcade. The canons would have sat at tables ranged around the side walls, with the prior seated on a raised platform or dais at the east end. In the south wall there would have been a pulpit in which one of the canons would have stood and read from a suitable book during meals, which were eaten in silence. To the south-west of the building are a series of low walls showing the position of the kitchen buildings that served the refectory. The main kitchen is a square building with traces of a central hearth and an oven in the south wall. Attached to its south side is another building which may have formed lodgings for some of the priory servants such as the cooks.

*Move to the south towards the stone drainage channel of the latrine.*

## Latrine

The latrine, or reredorter, was attached to the canons' dormitory with the seats on the floor above. In its basement is a great stone-lined drain which was flushed by running water to carry away the waste. This drain starts high up the hillside and runs in a long curving arc serving a series of buildings along its way, including the infirmary hall.

*Move up the far side of this eastern range of buildings. Take the passage through its basement then walk up the hill to the infirmary hall.*

## Infirmary

At the far end is a series of ruined buildings, which included the infirmary hall. This provided for sick, old or infirm canons and was a rest place for all the canons after the regular bleeding they were subjected to for health reasons. The regime in the infirmary was less rigorous than that of the cloister, and meat formed a regular part of the diet. Though ruined to a low level, it is possible to recognise that the hall was a large building divided by two rows of piers into five bays. On its east side there was a doorway covered by a porch, and a fireplace set in the adjoining bay. Originally it would have been divided up by timber screens into cubicles for the residents, though only the base of one screen now survives. On the north side there is another smaller building

with traces of a fireplace, perhaps the residence of the infirmarer. It is thought that part of this range provided accommodation for the retired priors of the house. To the south of this hall there is a complicated series of rooms which it is thought formed the prior's lodging, and a misericord hall, with a kitchen on its east side. The misericord was a special refectory for eating meat, because although from the fourteenth century the canons were allowed to eat meat on a regular basis, this had to be cooked in a separate kitchen and eaten in a separate refectory. Most monasteries either converted existing buildings or constructed new ones in order to locate the misericord where it was most convenient.

Above this, on the first floor, was the prior's residence, which would have consisted of a hall and bedroom with a study and private chapel.

*The long drain of the latrine running along the south side of the site*

*The remains of the infirmary hall from the north*

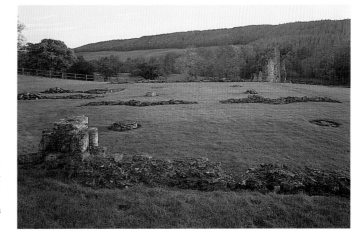

*Walk back to the entrance along the eastern perimeter of the site, behind the church. As you leave the monastic precinct, take the opportunity to turn and study the impressive gatehouse.*

## Gatehouse

The great gatehouse formed the main entrance into the priory and was built during the late thirteenth or early four-teenth century. It has a wide carriage arch, surmounted by a very decorative

*The decorative north front of the gatehouse*

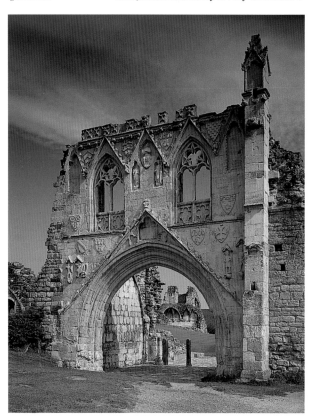

# ❖ THE HE

The gatehouse to the priory was rebuilt in the late thirteenth century. Its outer face was richly decorated with fine figure sculpture, and with the coats of arms of important patrons. Originally, the figures and shields would have been painted.

**The coats of arms**

1   de Clare
2   The arms of England
3   de Roos of Helmsley (principal patrons of the priory)
4   Vaux
5   Espec (founder of the priory)
6   Fitz-Ralph
7   Scrope
8-9   de Roos of Helmsley
10   de Fortibus

**The figure groups**

11   St Philip
12   Christ
13   St Bartholomew
14   George and the Dragon
15   The Crucifixion (now missing)
16   David and Goliath

# LDRY OF THE GATEHOUSE ❖

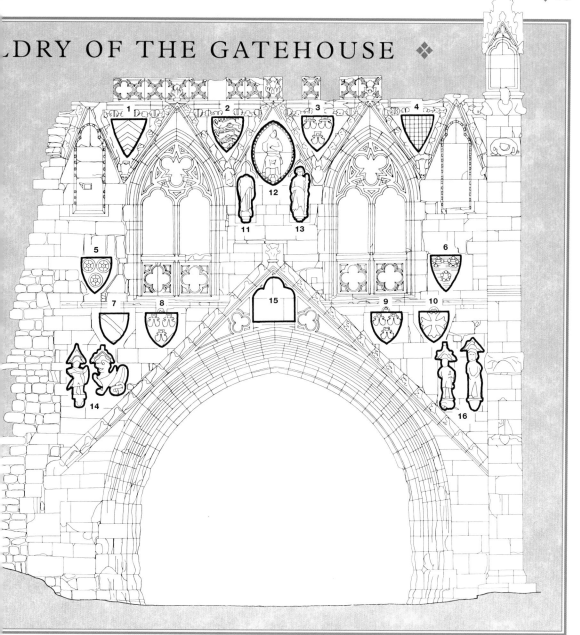

*The two Kentish-style windows in the gatehouse are like this one at Whitby Abbey*

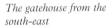

*The gatehouse from the south-east*

pointed gable, around which is ranged a series of shields bearing the arms of the noble patrons with which the priory was associated. These include those of the main patrons, the de Roos family (see Page 20). The shields are made to look as if they are hanging on hooks fastened to the wall.

The upper part of the wall is divided into five bays by crocketed gables. Within these are statue niches or windows, placed alternately. The central bay has three niches for statues, with a figure of Christ in majesty in the centre. The window divisions or tracery form pointed, star-shapes. This design is known as Kentish Style, and also occurs in the north wall of the church at Whitby Abbey. Above is a parapet with the remains of crenellations.

Flanking the entrance arch on the south side is a buttress which has a fine ornamented pinnacle or finial. This was one of a pair, but the corresponding northern buttress has been lost. The display of heraldry reflects a new fashion of the time, for architectural works to display the arms of the patrons associated with the institution. Similar hanging shields can be seen in the contemporary work in the nave of York Minster and the east end of Gisborough Priory. While acting as a decorative scheme, it also clearly declared to the outside world the association of the priory with rich and powerful families to whom it might turn in times of trouble. The gate passage was stone vaulted in two bays with the gates on the inner arch. On either side of the gatehouse, and continued in a chamber over the gate passage, was a series of ground and first-floor rooms thought to have served as accommodation for guests. Each room was provided with a fireplace and separate latrine.

*This is the end of the tour.*

# HISTORY OF
# THE PRIORY

## THE AUGUSTINIAN ORDER

The early years of the twelfth century saw a great revival of interest in the monastic way of life, and great changes in the established patterns of monastic settlement in Europe. New monastic orders were established and new religious houses spread like a tidal wave across the Continent. One of the first of the new orders was that of St Augustine. Following a regime that was less strict than the Benedictine Rule, the new order consisted of priests rather than monks, and its members were known as canons. They lived a communal life that was very similar to that of the Benedictines, but some of them also served as priests in certain parish churches.

The layout and design of Augustinian monasteries also basically followed that of the Benedictine plan, but the communities, and therefore the monasteries, tended to be smaller, and less expensive to maintain. However, there were notable exceptions

such as Bridlington, Gisborough and Thornton, as well as Kirkham, which rivalled even the largest Benedictine and Cistercian houses in size and wealth.

The first house of the order in England was that at St Botolph's Priory in Colchester, founded in 1100. From here, the order soon spread, and in Yorkshire, Bridlington was founded in 1113, Nostell in 1114 and Gisborough in 1119.

*St Augustine of Hippo, the leading fifth-century bishop whose writings formed the basis for the Augustinian rule*

BRIDGEMAN ART LIBRARY

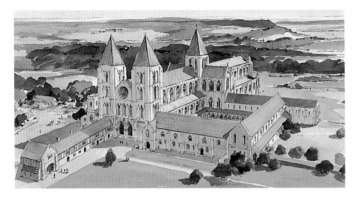

*Reconstruction of Gisborough, one of the largest Augustinian priories, by Terry Ball*

# THE FOUNDING OF KIRKHAM

The founder of Kirkham was Walter l'Espec, who had recently been given lands by the king. The first prior was William, rector of Garton, and the founder's uncle. He was also a canon of Nostell, which suggests that Nostell Priory was the founding house. As a result of the Augustinian interest in serving churches, the foundation grant included, besides Kirkham, seven churches and twenty caracutes (about 2080 acres or 42 hectares) of land, together with other properties which included the founder's houses in York. Altogether it was a generous grant, and it has been suggested that the community numbered around twenty-six canons.

Kirkham was established in about 1122 on a site which almost certainly had an existing church dating from the late Saxon period. The use of existing religious sites for new monastic foundations seems to have been common in this area, and indicates that the introduction of the Augustinians was seen at the time as a reform of the existing religious structure in Yorkshire. The reforms were actively promoted by the Archbishop of York.

*Plans of the early churches at Kirkham*

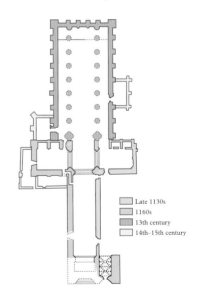

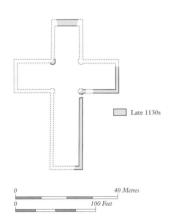

Late 1130s

0 — 40 Metres
0 — 100 Feet

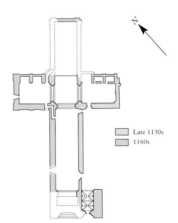

Late 1130s
1160s

Late 1130s
1160s
13th century
14th–15th century

The priory prospered and was probably soon able to start building in stone. However the attention of its patron, Walter l'Espec, soon became drawn to the other great contemporary reforming religious movement, the Cistercians, and in 1131 he established a new house of that order at Rievaulx, much closer than'Kirkham to his castle at Helmsley.

It may have been with some unease that the Kirkham canons viewed the establishment of this potentially rival house, particularly as it received grants of land which bordered their own. If this was the case, their fears were soon to be justified, for the establishment of Rievaulx made a huge impact upon the religious life of the north of England, with calls for reform in several monasteries. This soon reached a climax at St Mary's Abbey in York, where a group of the Benedictine monks, dissatisfied with the way the rule at St Mary's was being administered, had a violent quarrel with their abbot. With the

help of Archbishop Thurstan, they defected from St Mary's and founded another Cistercian house at Fountains, near Ripon. This set a precedent which seems to have influenced events at Kirkham shortly afterwards.

## DISSENT WITHIN THE COMMUNITY

Soon after 1132, Waltheof, stepson of King David of Scotland, and a friend of Walter l'Espec, became Kirkham's third prior. Waltheof and some of his canons became strongly influenced by the Cistercians of Rievaulx, and, between 1135 and 1139, an attempt was made, probably by l'Espec, to convert Kirkham to a Cistercian house. Unfortunately this seems to have split the community at Kirkham, as some of the canons did not agree with the proposal. An agreement survives by which these canons were to be relocated to a new site at Linton on Ouse where they were to be provided with new buildings comparable to those existing at Kirkham. They were to take with them all the coloured glass from the windows, as well as vestments, plate, utensils and books, leaving in place simple plain glass and a single bell. In the event, the agreement fell through, and the canons remained at Kirkham.

Waltheof seems to have been slow in deciding whether to join the Cistercians or not, for he led a new

*The ruins of Rievaulx, the great Cistercian abbey of the north*

*Reconstruction drawing of the Cistercian monks in the church at Rievaulx, by Peter Dunn*

*The ruins of Helmsley Castle today – home of the de Roos lords in the twelfth century*

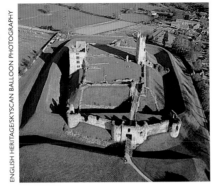

ENGLISH HERITAGE/SKYSCAN BALLOON PHOTOGRAPHY

Augustinian settlement to Thornton in North Lincolnshire in 1139, and only returned to Kirkham at the canons' request. Eventually he left Kirkham to join the Cistercians and became abbot of Warden (Rievaulx's daughter house), and subsequently of Melrose in Scotland, which had been founded by his stepfather. His reputation and sanctity were such that he was eventually recognised as a saint, and his tomb in the chapter house of Melrose became an object of pilgrimage. The division within the community at Kirkham was not without compensation, for it prompted l'Espec to issue a second foundation charter which confirmed and added substantially to his earlier endowments.

Despite the charter evidence, it seems clear that there was little animosity between the two monasteries, and in 1141 the Kirkham community joined ranks with those at Rievaulx

*A twelfth-century seal of Kirkham Priory*

to dispute the election of William Fitzherbert as Archbishop of York. Indeed, it is thought by some that Waltheof was considered by the dissenting parties as a rival candidate, though his connections with the Scottish royal house seem to have weighed against him. The appeal against the archbishop's election involved journeying to Rome to present the case in person to the Pope. The dispute dragged on for several years, and when it was resolved, Waltheof had converted to the Cistercians, become Abbot of Warden, and was not considered as a candidate. Henry Murdac, the energetic abbot of Fountains Abbey, was elected archbishop.

## THE DE ROOS FAMILY

Just before his death in 1155, l'Espec joined the Cistercians at Rievaulx where he was buried. His estates passed through his sisters to the de Roos who became the new lords of Helmsley and patrons of the priory. The house seems to have prospered for most of the twelfth century, a period which saw substantial rebuilding of the church. In the thirteenth century, the presbytery of Kirkham became the burial chamber of the family, many of the de Roos lords being buried in the area surrounding the high altar. The church was massively enlarged by the addition of a magnificent new

BRITISH LIBRARY

presbytery, and it seems that this grand rebuilding was intended to encompass the whole church and other parts of the priory buildings. Eventually however, the scheme was abandoned, and the turbulent years at the start of the fourteenth century meant that it was never resurrected.

## MONASTIC LIFE

Life at the priory followed a regular routine of seven services a day, with additional services on feast days and at the great festivals of Easter and Christmas. The church was provided with many altars at which the canons celebrated mass. The daily routine was not quite as rigorous as that of the Cistercians or Benedictines, and some of the canons were expected to serve as priests at churches held by the priory. These canons thus obtained a break from the monotony of monastic life, though the majority of the churches held by the priory were served by vicars, in return for a regular fee or stipend. This was advantageous to the priory which took the surplus parochial income for itself. Thus, in 1291, around two-thirds of the priory income was derived from churches. This was known as its 'spiritualities' as opposed to the 'temporalities' or income derived from its lands. By the time of the Dissolution of the Monasteries in the 1530s, this income balance had changed to around half from each source.

As an institution, the priory had many rights and privileges which it was quick to defend if it was thought that infringements had occurred. This could even extend to taking legal actions against patrons, as demonstrated by a case brought in the king's court in 1257, against a William de Roos. William was again sued in 1261 over hunting rights in Helmsley woods and moor. It seems clear that he had been trying to alienate rights granted to the priory by Walter l'Espec a hundred and thirty years before. The priory won each case, and it cost Lord Roos additional lands and privileges to settle the matter. Despite these legal wrangles, William was still allowed to be buried before the high altar of the priory church.

*Two monks reading, from a medieval manuscript illustration*

*The de Roos tomb in Temple Church, London*

*Reconstruction drawing by Terry Ball of the prior's hall and infirmary at Kirkham*

Though it was an independent priory, Kirkham was subject to the discipline of the archbishops of York, and their visitation registers show how the priory was plunged into serious debt. In 1280 the finances were in order, but in 1314 there were deficiencies in the chapter house, dormitory and infirmary which required repair, and there were heavy debts. In 1321 John de Yarm was elected prior, and the archbishop noted that the debts now totalled £843-15s-91/2d. An explanation shows that the bulk of the debt had

accumulated through non-payment of rents since 1314 from the priory's Northumberland estates, valued at 1000 marks (£670) per year. Presumably these estates had largely been lost or laid waste during the war between Edward ll and Robert the Bruce which culminated in the Scottish victory at Bannockburn. To help pay off the debt, the prior had resorted to selling corrodies, a form of medieval pension scheme. By 1357 the debt had grown to £1000, and the archbishop allowed the dispersal of some of the Kirkham canons to other houses to reduce it. Northumberland was regained in the 1350s but it would have taken considerable time to restore the estates to their former prosperity.

The position of prior could prove a rewarding situation. As head of the community, the prior lived in a separate household with his own servants, and on retirement he was well provided for. Records show that prior John de Elveley retired in 1310 with a pension of £20 per year and lodgings close to the infirmary. This included a garden adjoining his chamber and a second garden near the river Derwent. He was to have fourteen white loaves and fourteen gallons of better ale weekly, with soup, relishes and salted meat. His companion received seven loaves and seven gallons of good ale and was provided with a chaplain, esquire, a cook and two boys as servants. He also had two horses (a palfrey and a sumpter), with additional horses for the servants. Clearly the life of a retired prior was one of ease, though ex-prior John had problems getting the priory to honour the agreement, and eventually the archbishop issued an order to moderate the pension.

In 1308, the Archbishop had cause to enquire about one canon who had apparently been imprisoned in the priory gaol for over seventeen years because he had forged the priory seals, fraudulently obtained money, and then absconded to lead a riotous life. After being chased across England he was finally caught. Still unrepentant, he was tried and sentenced by the Prior's Court.

## THE DISSOLUTION OF THE MONASTERIES

By 1535, King Henry VIII had established himself as Head of the English Church and ordered a survey of the income of the church, known as the *Valor Ecclesiasticus*, in which Kirkham was assessed as having a net annual income of £269-5s-9d. Henry then decided to close down all those monasteries with an annual value of less than £200, and, in the process, gain all their income and property for himself. Kirkham thus escaped the first round of monastic closures in 1536. However the King soon decided to close the wealthier religious houses too, and in December 1538 the prior of Kirkham, and seventeen of its canons, signed the deed of surrender in exchange for pensions. The prior was awarded £50 per year with smaller amounts to each canon.

*Henry VIII depicted in an initial letter, from the document containing the valuation of all church property of 1535*

*Old woodcut of Kirkham from Gent's* History of Ripon

*Part of an engraving of Kirkham by Samuel and Nathaniel Buck, 1721*

As they were priests, most of the dispossessed canons probably continued in some form of religious life, and we know that some of them continued to serve the same churches that had been held by the priory. The last prior, John Kildwick, continued living on his pension in the Kirkham area and, in his will made in 1552, left bequests to the surrounding villages, and gold angels to five of his former colleagues. The wills of two of the former canons show that they wished to be buried in the priory church and they also made bequests of books and caps to former colleagues. Clearly the sense of community and friendship felt by the canons continued long after the priory had been dissolved.

The monastic buildings would have been stripped of all the plate and valuable metals such as the bells and lead from the roofs. Anything of saleable value would have been salvaged and disposed of by the king's agents, to maximise the profit from the site. The buildings may have been slighted (purposely damaged) by pulling down the vaults and the church tower, to ensure that they could never be used again.

The site soon passed out of crown ownership when it was sold, in May 1540, to Henry Knevett. According to local tradition, stone was taken from the site to build nearby Howsham Hall. Mid seventeenth-century drawings of the site show that by then the buildings had already reached nearly their present state of ruination. More of the east wall of the church was standing at that time, but unfortunately it collapsed soon after.

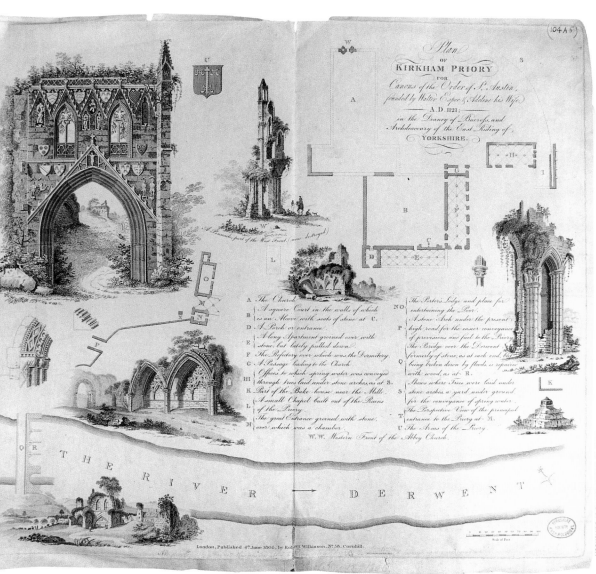

*Plan and detailed drawings of the Priory by Robert Wilkinson, 1806*

*Watercolour of the Gatehouse at Kirkham by John Sell Cotman (1782–1842)*

*The river at Kirkham was a busy tourist attraction in the 1920s and '30s*

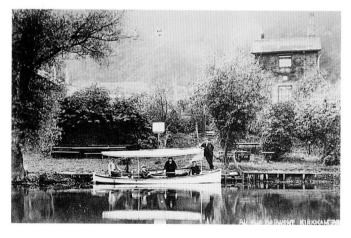

## Recent History

Some excavation of the presbytery was undertaken by the famous late-Victorian archaeologist, Sir William St. John Hope, but unfortunately he never published his discoveries. The ruins had become much overgrown, but nineteenth-century photographs show the cloister laid out as a tennis court, with rustic benches provided for visitors.

In the 1920s and '30s, Kirkham was a busy tourist attraction and the river was much used for recreation. There were two busy boat yards (with cafés and shops) and a regular traffic of boats up and down the river.

Following the First World War, the site was transferred to the guardianship of the Office of Works. Conservation of the remaining walls now commenced to ensure their long-term preservation, as well as excavations to clear the debris of collapsed buildings and expose the buried walls.

During the Second World War, Kirkham was used as a training and testing site by the military, in preparation for the D-Day landings. We know that a very large hole (the size of a swimming pool) was excavated adjacent to the priory ruins. This was used to test new waterproofing techniques for military vehicles. The base appears to have been quite high-profile and something of a secret, but both Churchill and the Royal family came to visit the site during this period.

The site is now in the care of English Heritage.

*Nineteenth-century photographs showing the cloister being used as a tennis court (above) and rustic benches installed in the laver arches for spectators (below)*

YORKSHIRE ARCHAEOLOGICAL SOCIETY

YORKSHIRE ARCHAEOLOGICAL SOCIETY

## Acknowledgements

In preparing a guide such as this, it is inevitable that a writer has to draw on the work of previous authors. I would therefore like to acknowledge the contribution of, and express my debt to, the late Sir Charles Peers, who wrote the earlier guidebook to Kirkham, and Dr Glyn Coppack who has studied the remains of the priory in depth. In particular, I have drawn heavily on the published and unpublished works of Dr Janet Burton who has done more than anyone else to reveal the history of the canons of Kirkham.

## Bibliography

*Kirkham Priory from Foundation to Dissolution*, Janet Burton. University of York Borthwick Paper No 86, 1995
*Kirkham Priory: The Architecture and Archaeology of an Augustinian House* Glyn Coppack, Stuart Harrison, and Colin Hayfield.
*Journal of the British Archaeological Association*, Volume CXLVIII 1995, p55-136

# PLAN OF THE PRIORY

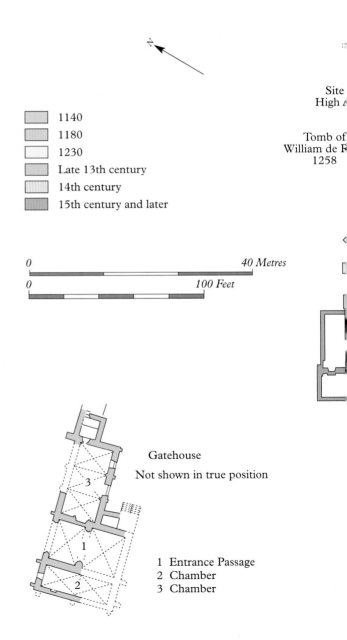

1140

1180

1230

Late 13th century

14th century

15th century and later

0                                        40 Metres

0                          100 Feet

Site
High A

Tomb of
William de F
1258

Gatehouse
Not shown in true position

1 Entrance Passage
2 Chamber
3 Chamber